Miscarriage
A Shattered Dream

Sherokee Ilse
Linda Hammer Burns

Acknowledgments

We appreciate and want to thank our husbands, David and Sheldon, who supported us, inspired us, and critiqued our work. We also thank them for taking over family duties while we were intent on this project.

We would also like to express our gratitude to the following people who contributed to the writing, editing, and content of this book:

Marge Aderly
Beth Bailey, MD
Shari Baldinger, MS
Steven Blake
Sheldon R. Burns, MD
Rita Duncan
David Dunsworth, MD
Diane Eggen, RN
Susan Erling
Marlene Fondrick, RN, MSN

Gerald Jensen, MD
Patricia Irwin Johnston
Barb Korsell, RN
Gail Kouri, RN
Jo-el Quinn-Kroening
Sue Lamoreaux, MSW
Judy Leathem, RN
Martha Lofstrom
Sharon Sinclair, MA
Mary Sommerfeld

Cover Design: Scott Barsuhn
            Barsuhn Design
            Bob Wasulik

Editors: Debra Pysno
         Marty Heiberg
         Nancy Stesin

Typesetting: deRuyter Nelson Publications, Inc.
Printing: Lakeland Press

Copyright © 1985 by Sherokee Ilse and Linda Hammer Burns
Updated in 2000, 2002, 2006, 2014

For additional copies write to:
    Wintergreen Press
    801 Twelve Oaks Center Drive Suite 803
    Wayzata, MN 55391
    (952) 476-1303
    www.wintergreenpress.com

ISBN 0-9609456-3-6

Dedication

We lovingly dedicate this book to our children,
Kellan and Trevor, Alicen and Evan,
to our miscarried babies
and
to all the families whose dreams have been shattered,
whose pregnancies have ended prematurely,
and to all of the babies
who will never grace this earth with their presence.

We gratefully acknowledge the following for use of their poems and prose included throughout this book:

Page ii   Dreams, Copyright©1932, Alfred A. Knopf, Inc.
           Renewed 1960 by Langston Hughes from *Don't You Turn Back*, Langston
           Hughes. Reprinted by permission of the publisher.

Page 1   *Blackberry Winter*, by Margaret Mead. Reprinted by permission of
           William Morrow & Company, Inc.

Page 4   "But it hurts…Differently" from *Living—when a loved one has died* by
           Earl Grollman. Copyright©1977 by Earl A. Grollman. Reprinted by
           permission of Beacon Press.

Page 7   Reprinted from *Baby Care* by permission of Pocket Books, a Division of
           Simon & Schuster, Inc. Copyright©by Dr. Benjamin Spock.

Page 21   *Desiderata*, by Max Ehrmann, Copyright©1972. Reprinted by permission
           of The Crown Publishing Group.

Page 25   Reprinted by permission of Simon & Schuster, Inc. Copyright©by Will
           and Ariel Durant.

Page 26   "A Prayer for Baby" Reprinted from *On Children and Death*,
           Copyright©by Elisabeth Kubler-Ross with permission.

Page 27   "Men" from *"New and Collected Poems"* 1917-1976 by Archibald
           MacLeish. Copyright©1976 by Archibald MacLeish. Reprinted by
           permission of Houghton Mifflin Company.

Page 30   Song from *Ice Castles*, by Marvin Hamlisch. Reprinted by permission of
           Screen Gems, EMI Music, Inc.

Page 40   "The Second Sowing" Copyright©1948 by Anne Morrow Lindbergh.
           Reprinted from *The Unicorn and Other Poems*, by permission of Pantheon
           Books, a Division of Random House, Inc.

Page 41   "Adoption" by Fleur Heyliger. Copyright©1952 The Curtis Publishing
           Company. Reprinted with permission from The *Saturday Evening Post*.

Page 42   *Marriage Without Children*, by Diana Burgwyn, Copyright©1981 Diana
           Burgwyn. Reprinted by permission of Harper & Row Co., Publishing, Inc.

Page 43   Quote by Margot Fromer. Reproduced by permission from Fromer,
           Margot Joan: *Ethical issues in sexuality and reproduction*, St. Louis,
           1983, The C.V. Mosby Company.

Table of Contents

About the Authors

I was always glad that I was a girl. As a girl, I knew that someday I would have children. My closest models, my mother and my grandmother, had both had children and also used their minds and had careers in the public world. So I had no doubt that whatever career I might choose, I would have children too.

Margaret Mead

Sherokee

Children were always in our plan for marriage, even though this was mostly unspoken between David and me. After five years of marriage, we agreed to stop using birth control and let what was to happen, happen.

When our pregnancy was confirmed nine months later we were both excitedly anticipating the whole adventure. We told everyone we could think of about the pregnancy almost as soon as we knew, only to find two weeks later that we were experiencing a miscarriage. We felt total shock. How could this happen to us? The cool reception we received in the Emergency Room did not make it easier to accept. We each had many feelings but we did not discuss them at the time. Nor did we receive encouragement from those around us to do so. We were told "Get pregnant again soon; you'll feel better."

I remember rationalizing the miscarriage, thinking it was probably for the best. Besides, I was building my career and was very interested in long distance running. So I felt the miscarriage gave me more time to pursue those interests. Yet as every May rolls around I can't help but remember my miscarried baby: a birthday uncelebrated, a void in our lives.

It wasn't until a year and half later, when our son, Brennan, was stillborn that we went back and discussed what had happened and our feelings about the miscarriage. In some ways we regrieved that baby and loss too, but in a healthy and positive way.

One can never anticipate how one would deal with a loss in the future, but I think that if we were to experience a miscarriage today we would do things much differently. For example, I believe we might name the baby and have a memorial service.

We feel extremely fortunate and thankful to have two healthy sons, Kellan and Trevor. Yet our lives are different, and in many ways better, because of the loss of our other children. We realize what true miracles birth and life are and believe we have a better perspective about parenting because of our experiences.

1

****

As a result of her own experience and her desire to help others with similar losses, Sherokee wrote *Empty Arms:Coping with Miscarriage, Stillbirth and Infant Death.* She is a nationally known speaker on the subject of perinatal loss and has written several booklets and articles on the topic, including the books/bookletslets: *Giving Care, Taking Care, Single Parents,* and *Ectopic Pregnancy/Blighted Ovum.* A certified teacher and President of Wintergreen Press, Sherokee has a degree in psychology and sociology from Hamline Univeristy in St. Paul, Minnesota.

Linda

Like Margaret Mead and Sherokee, children were always a part of our future and our plans. In fact, Sheldon and I often debated, "How many children?" simply assuming that there would be children.

We had been married two years when we decided to get pregnant during a six-week trip to Europe. How pleased and excited we were when we discovered that I was pregnant. When I began to spot a few days after our return, we thought it was part of pregnancy. Miscarriage was not in our vocabulary, let alone in our experience. The days that followed were tense and confusing. The limbo ended with a negative pregnancy test and a D & C. The confusion that dominated those early days continued for quite some time. We were each disappointed and hurt, angry and bewildered, and we did not know how to share those feelings with each other. I vividly remember Sheldon's anger, which I interpreted as anger at me. His feelings and my reaction to them created a distance between us that need not have been, had we been able to communicate more openly.

Although the miscarriage was difficult, what followed for us was even more difficult. We could not get pregnant again. We began a regime of temperature charts, medications, and emotional ups and downs as we tried to capture something that seemed so easy for others, yet so elusive for us. As the months and years passed, the miscarried child that might have been seemed even more valuable and important.

Since then we have experienced the birth and lives of two children, Alicen and Evan, as well as other pregnancy losses. Through it all—infertility, pregnancy loss, and parenting—we have learned a great deal about ourselves and our marriage. In many ways the miscarriages and infertility pulled us apart. Yet, sharing them provided the basis for us to work together to pull together. We now value our past for what it waas given us. We value our children in a different way. And we value each other and the life we have bade together out of the ashes of our past.

*****

Motivated by her experience with infertility and pregnancy loss, Linda was co-founder of RESOLVE of the Twin Cities, a local chapter of the national support group for couples. Linda earned a Masters Degree in counseling psychology from the College of St. Thomas in St. Paul, Minnesota. She is a family therapist specializing in the issues of infertility, pregnancy loss, and parenting after a loss. A frequent speaker and instructor, Linda has written several articles and booklets on infertility, pregnancy loss, adoption, and the impact of reproductive failure on parenting. She also has a special interest in the ethical dilemmas of reproductive technology. Ms. Hammer Burns has a Bachelor's Degree in philosophy and religion from Hamline University in St. Paul, Minnesota and has her doctorate from the University of Minnesota.

Introduction

But It Hurts...Differently

*There is no way to predict
How you will feel.*

*The reactions of grief
Are not like recipes,
With given ingredients,
And certain results.*

*Each person mourns in a
different way.*

*You may cry hysterically,
Or
You may remain outwardly controlled,
Showing little emotion.*

*You may lash out in anger
Against your family and friends,
Or
You may express your graditude
For their concern and dedication.*

*You may be calm one moment—
In turmoil the next.*

*Reactions are varied and
Contradictory.*

*Grief is universal.
At the same time it
Is extremely personal.*

Heal in your own way.

Earl A. Grollman

Miscarriage—a shattered dream. The child that was to have been is no more; the end of a pregnancy. Even though you may have been pregnant for only a short time, your hopes and plans for a new and changed life were real.

Miscarriage is one of the most misunderstood, as well as the most frequent, losses. Statistics are not kept, but it's estimated that close to 800,000 families in the United States experience a miscarriage each year. This is approximately 20-30% of all documented conceptions. Miscarriage is a loss that is often minimized and overlooked because it occurs so often and so early in pregnancy.

Miscarriage is an event that triggers emotional reactions in all those involved. Yet these reactions can vary greatly from person to person in their meaning and intensity. Whether the child was anxiously awaited, reluctantly accepted, or unexpected, feelings of loss occur as a result of this sudden and unplanned change. You might feel bewildered, alone, or surprised by your emotions after your miscarriage. There is no typical response to miscarriage. Some people accept it as another life experience, deal with it, and move on. Others feel upset and unsettled, while still others are devastated by the strong impact it has on them.

You and your partner might have similar or quite different reactions. There is no sure predictor and you will need to talk about how each of you is feeling to determine the similarities and differences. The different responses to miscarriage might be better understood by looking at the differences in parents' reactions to the pregnancy and baby. Some parents planned for the baby, some did not. Some parents wanted the baby they were expecting, some did not. If you were trying to conceive for a long time or found yourself very excited at the prospect of a new life, miscarriage can be a devastating blow. Often feelings are mixed. You might have been pleased because you were able to conceive, yet not ready to be a parent.

If you had symptoms such as bleeding over several weeks, the miscarriage might be a relief, in that it brings to a close something that has been threatening and worrisome. If this was an unwanted or unplanned pregnancy you might feel either relief, discontentment or sadness, depending on your hopes, plans, and feelings about the pregnancy.

Repeated pregnancy losses might cause more frustration and despair with each subsequent loss. Or you might find that since you know what to expect, each pregnancy loss that follows is actually easier.

Since there are no right or wrong reactions after miscarriage, it should be clear that there is a wide range of responses. To illustrate the diverse reactions possible after such a loss, here is a sampling of peoples' feelings about their miscarriage:

"We never felt the kicks or watched the physical changes as our baby grew, but nevertheless we felt an intense loss and emptiness after the miscarriage."

"I had feelings of guilt, bitterness, and resentment. Some days were good, others were bad."

"I don't understand why my wife feels so badly. It's one of those things. We can try again right away."

"I was disappointed that I would not be able to wear my new maternity clothes and I was upset for my parents because it was their first grandchild."

"I was sad but also kind of relieved because we already had three children and were having trouble supporting them as it was."

"I don't think I ever really 'recovered' or 'accepted' my miscarriage, but I was able to put my life in perspective and find a 'new normal' for myself."

"I felt a little disappointed. I hadn't really realized I was pregnant and we weren't really ready for it, so it was both bad and good. I do wonder if I will feel worse about this later, though."

"We had wanted this baby so badly. We planned, and saved, and were so ready. It never occurred to either one of us that this could happen. I still can't believe it."

"After so many years of trying, when I finally did become pregnant it was like a dream. We'd had so much trouble getting pregnant, it never occurred to us that pregnancy could go wrong, that something could happen after I got pregnant. It seems like the last straw."

"Everyone kept asking 'How's Joanie doing?' Nobody ever asked me how I was doing and I was doing awful."

Family and friends might make light of the miscarriage, not really knowing the full impact it has on you. Or they might expect you to be very upset when you actually feel accepting of what has happened. If you don't feel others are helpful or giving you what you need, you will probably have to speak up and share with them what you are feeling and what you want from them.

Whether you have a strong emotional reaction to your miscarriage or not, this book can help you understand yourself and the point of view of others. Use the appropriate sections as a springboard for discussion or a source of information. Remember that you need not experience this in the same way as anyone else. You have a right to your feelings and needs, as do the other people with whom you interact.

For the sake of simplification we will use the term miscarriage to include all early pregnancy losses, including ectopic and molar pregnancies. We will also refer to "partner" throughout the book. Many who read this will be single women, whom we want to feel included. Yes, this book is for you too. If you aren't married or don't have a steady partner, please think of a close friend or family member when we talk about partners. If there are sections that don't apply to you, skim over them.

We are very sorry that you have experienced a miscarriage. We both wish you well as you move through this experience, try to put some meaning to it, and weave it into the fabric of your life. We have walked a similar path. We know some of what you are going through and we hope that what we have written in this book will offer you some comfort and guidance.

1

Attachment: The Beginning of a Relationship

Of course, parents don't have children because they want to be martyrs, at least they shouldn't. They have them because they love children and want some of their very own. They also love children because they remember being loved so much by their parents in their childhood.

Dr. Benjamin Spock

Maybe you knew you were pregnant for only a few days or maybe you knew for weeks, even months. Perhaps you are wondering if this was a life worth mourning and missing. The answer to that can only be found within you, but it may be easier to find after reflecting on your feelings about your pregnancy and baby.

Attachment is the emotional bond of preparing and caring for your baby. Only you know how much this pregnancy meant, how many plans or dreams you had for your baby and family. Your feelings of attachment for your baby will influence your feelings about your miscarriage. You might feel minor disappointment, intense grief, or something in between.

Did you think of this as a baby rather than just a pregnancy? Did you have the nursery planned or prepared? Were you picturing yourself as a parent? If you had plans, dreams, and hopes for this baby, it makes sense that you may feel very sad and disappointed for what can no longer be at this time.

On the other hand, maybe you were not ready for this pregnancy. Did you feel hesitant about having a baby or have a difficult time accepting the reality of the pregnancy? If so, the miscarriage may have left you feeling emotionally untouched, vaguely discontented, or confused. You might have wondered, even though you knew it to be foolish, if your feelings of ambivalence toward the pregnancy somehow caused the miscarriage. It is important to realize that even though you may not be distraught about the miscarriage, you may still experience some feelings of loss or uneasiness.

By understanding some of the dynamics of preparation for pregnancy and parenthood, it could be easier to understand how you and others react to the miscarriage. Attachment, the growing bond of caring, is the beginning of the relationship between parent and child. Most people prepare for parenthood long before they become parents. In childhood, boys and girls try on the roles and behaviors of their parents and the adults around them. Children play with dolls and play house, take care of younger siblings or pets, and imagine themselves as grown-ups with children of their own. They assume that parenthood will be a part of their adulthood.

Often part of choosing a partner in adulthood is imagining that person as the parent of their children. Later on in anticipation of parenthood, couples usually make space in their lives and their relationship for the baby that will arrive someday. This continues when a couple decides to have a child or when a pregnancy is confirmed.

Preparation for parenthood is a part of a healthy bonding process that often occurs beyond your awareness. You and your partner may have prepared yourselves without realizing it. You may have done this when you considered names for your baby, thought about daycare, or planned for future holidays with your new family member. Perhaps you were able to see your baby moving inside your uterus through an ultrasound examination. This may have made the existence of the baby more real to you and your partner.

Your feelings of emptiness may be more understandable if you recognize that your relationship with your child has not been as brief as you may have thought. Not all of your feelings are from this day or month.

2

Common Questions and Concerns

Nothing in life is to be feared, it is only to be understood.

Marie Curie

What is a miscarriage?

Miscarriage is the term commonly used to describe the unplanned end of a pregnancy before a baby can live on its own. The medical term for this, *spontaneous abortion,* means the termination of a pregnancy by natural causes before twenty weeks of pregnancy and before the baby can live outside the uterus. When a baby dies before birth but after twenty weeks' gestation it is called a *stillbirth.* This book deals only with pregnancy loss that occurs prior to twenty weeks.

Accurate statistics on the incidence of miscarriage are almost impossible to arrive at for a number of reasons. One is that most states do not require that such records be kept. Another is that miscarriage is most likely to occur during the first trimester (three months) of pregnancy, often before a woman realizes she is pregnant or before the pregnancy has been confirmed by a pregnancy test or a medical exam. It is currently estimated that 20 to 30% of all confirmed pregnancies and up to 50% or perhaps more of all conceptions end in miscarriage.

No two miscarriages are alike, even for the woman who has previously experienced one. A miscarriage may occur with a sudden loss of blood, with spotting, or with a heavier than normal period. Cramping may be unnoticeabale, mildly uncomfortable, or severe. A miscarriage may occur suddenly, with the complete passing of the baby or fetal tissue, or it may take place over several days or weeks. Medical attention will vary depending on the circumstances.   In some cases only a simple examination of the uterus may be necessary, while in others short hospitalization or surgery may be required. In all cases, medical follow-up is absolutely necessary.

What happens during a miscarriage?

Each miscarriage is unique and doesn't fit any predictable pattern. It might be helpful if you first understand the terms used to describe miscarriage. In this book, the term miscarriage will be used instead of the commonly accepted medical term, *abortion.*

Miscarriages are described as *threatened, inevitable, incomplete,* and *missed* (see diagram).

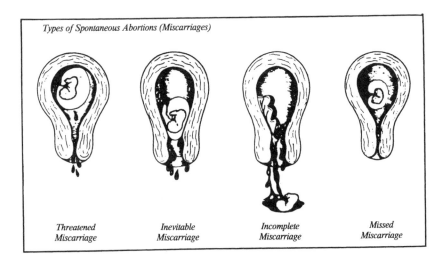

Types of Spontaneous Abortions (Miscarriages)

| Threatened Miscarriage | Inevitable Miscarriage | Incomplete Miscarriage | Missed Miscarriage |

A *threatened miscarriage* is diagnosed when there is staining (spotting) or bleeding, but the cervix is still closed. At this time a pregnancy test might be negative, indicating that the baby has died, or the test might be positive, meaning that the baby is still alive but for some reason there is bleeding.

An *inevitable miscarriage* usually means that bleeding has increased (usually it is bright red), the cervix is open, ready to pass the baby, and there is cramping.

An *incomplete miscarriage* means that the fetus has died and part of it or the placenta still remains inside the uterus.

A *missed miscarriage* means that the fetus has died but has failed to pass out of the uterus.

Another type of pregnancy loss results from ***ectopic pregnancy.*** An ectopic pregnancy is one that is located in any place other than the uterus (see diagram).

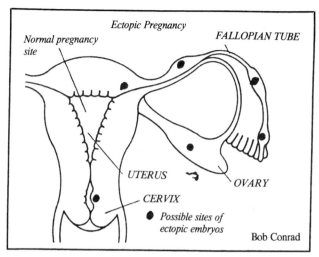

Ninety-five percent of all such pregnancies implant in a Fallopian tube, which explains the commonly used term "tubal pregnancy." Often the Fallopian tube must be surgically removed along with the fetus. Sometimes another organ, such as the uterus, has been ruptured by the pregnancy and must be removed. The removal of one Fallopian tube or the uterus can affect future fertility, which is often a concern to many couples. However, many women do go on to become pregnant and bear children after an ectopic pregnancy.

Ectopic pregnancy occurs in 2 to 3% of all conceptions. Once a woman has had an ectopic pregnancy her chances of having another are increased to as much as 1 in 10. Because of the possibility of internal bleeding from a ruptured tube, ovary, or uterus, an ectopic pregnancy is a medical emergency. This is often unknown to both the woman or her partner.

Symptoms such as dizziness, fainting, sharp pains in the abdomen, abdominal discomfort stronger than menstrual cramps, or vaginal bleeding or spotting, can be signs of internal bleeding and medical attention should be sought immediately.

Ectopic pregnancy is a unique type of pregnancy loss and your emotional responses may be complicated by your medical condition. You may feel very angry and not know why. The loss of the baby, although a source of sadness, may have been overshadowed by fears for your health or life. Those around you may be so relieved that you are alive that you receive little or no support for the loss of the baby. For you, the loss of all or part of your fertility may be the main concern. Whatever your response, it is important to remember that you are dealing with several issues and losses.

Another type of pregnancy loss is a ***molar pregnancy***, in which the baby dies or never develops while the placenta continues to grow. The uterus enlarges and the body responds as if a pregnancy were developing normally. Ultrasound or the lack of fetal

11

heart tones are signs that might indicate that this type of pregnancy has occurred.

Your medical caregiver might refer to molar pregnancy as trophoblastic disease or hydatidiform mole. This is usually a benign, but cancer-like, disease that can be effectively treated. However, it must be closely followed for several months after the placenta has been surgically removed.

You might have feelings of loss after a molar pregnancy, but be more alarmed about your health. You might also be concerned because your caregiver has recommended that another pregnancy be postponed for health reasons. It is important to recognize your increased need for support because you are dealing with two very important and sometimes separate issues.

What medical interventions will be recommended?

Some miscarriages require surgical intervention while others do not. In some cases, particularly those that are not medical emergencies, you might have choices about treatment and the surgical procedures used. Make certain that you and your partner or a family member fully understand the procedure being recommended and the expected outcome.

Before any treatment is recommended or begun, your medical caregiver may suggest blood tests or an ultrasound examination. Blood tests can determine if your body is still producing the hormones associated with pregnancy. Ultrasound uses high frequency sound waves to see the uterus, fetus, and placenta. Ultrasound may tell the caregiver where the pregnancy is located and if the baby is still alive.

If some tissue remains in the uterus and bleeding continues, your medical attendant might recommend the removal of the remaining tissue in order to prevent infection or futher bleeding. There are two methods of doing this: *suction curettage* and *dilation and curettage,* also known as D & C.

During a *suction curettage,* the cervix is dilated and the uterine contents are gently evacuated with a vacuum-like instrument. This procedure is usually done in an outpatient clinic or emergency room. It requires only local anesthesia, which is an injection of a numbing medication into the cervix.

A *D & C* is the manual opening of the cervix in order to curette or scrape the uterine lining. It is most often performed when the placenta has remained partly attached to the uterus or when the contents of the uterus must be removed in order to prevent further bleeding. This short procedure is performed under general anesthesia, usually lasts 15 to 25 minutes, and may require a minimal hospital stay.

What if I have Rh negative blood?

At the time of the miscarriage your medical attendant will probably test your blood for the Rh factor if you have not been tested earlier. If you are not tested, do ask about it. If you are Rh negative it is very important to obtain a RhoGAM injection. Having this injection as soon as possible after a miscarriage can help prevent antibody production in your body that can be harmful in subsequent pregnancies.

What options and decisions do I face?

Although the following options may not yet be widely practiced in our society, they are not so odd or unusual. In each case there is a rationale for why they might be helpful. If some of them feel right to you and are choices you want to consider—do so. If, on the other hand, you don't feel comfortable with some of them, don't feel pressured to consider them.

Whatever you choose, do what you and your partner believe is best for you. Use this opportunity to take some control of the situation by creating memories with which you can live.

Medical intervention. Depending on the kind of miscarriage you have experienced, you may have a choice about whether or not to have one of the medical procedures described on page 12. Some women prefer to wait, allowing their body the opportunity to expel the miscarried baby. This is something you should thoroughly discuss with your medical attendant because your decision can affect your physical health.

Partner present for the D & C or suction curettage. Having your partner or a support person beside you during the medical procedure might be comforting to you. It might help make the pregnancy and miscarriage more of a reality to your partner. In addition, you might find the procedure less threatening if a supportive, familiar person is nearby. Your partner can stand or sit by your head if there is concern about the blood or the procedure itself.

If this option is not offered, do not be afraid to make this request.

Seeing the baby or tissue. After a miscarriage, a ten-week-old fetus is sometimes recognizable as a very tiny human form. Sometimes seeing the baby or the tissue that is removed from the uterus helps affirm that there was a baby. It is a good idea to be prepared for seeing the baby by having someone describe it or by looking at pictures of babies of the same gestational age. Many parents find that what they imagined their baby looked like was far worse than the reality. Be aware that after a D & C or a suction curettage, the uterine contents might be difficult to distinguish as a baby.

Pictures of the baby or removed organs. Many physicians take photos of the baby or organs that have been surgically removed in order to make the loss more understandable and real for you. At first, it may be difficult to look at the pictures, but it can be reassuring to know they are there. Seeing pictures does help make a very unreal experience more tangible.

Holding or touching your baby. If your baby was old enough you might consider touching or holding it. It is likely that you and those around you might be concerned with the appearance of the baby. Many parents say that seeing, touching, or holding their baby helped validate their baby's existence. For many it is important in saying hello and goodbye.

Disposition of the baby's remains or the tissue. In most states, you have the right to your baby's remains, even after tests have been performed. You will need to inform your medical attendant or medical facility what you wish to be done with your baby's remains. You may choose to arrange for burial or cremation [see below] or you may choose to leave these arrangements to the hospital or medical facility.

The hospital might not tell you what choices you have and, in fact, might act as if it is their decision, not yours. Be sure to discuss this with them. You can request information about their procedures regarding disposition of the baby's remains. Once you have made your decision, you should be asked to sign a form indicating your choice.

Naming your baby. Giving your baby a name can be an intimate way of honoring your child, although you might choose not to remember your infant in this way. Naming can make the baby seem more real to you, your other children, and other family members. You might wish to give your child the name you used when referring to him or her during the pregnancy.

Baptism or Kaddish. Choosing to baptize your baby will depend on your religious beliefs and your personal needs. You might choose to baptize your miscarried baby even though it is not recognizable as a baby. This can be another means of confirming the personhood or reality of your infant. Anyone can baptize a baby, anywhere.

Another option is to have a prayer service or a simple blessing said for your baby. This can also serve as a meaningful ceremony. Jewish families can choose to say Kaddish for their babies as a special way of saying goodbye, even though this has not been done traditionally.

Memorial or funeral service or Shiva. Consider holding a memorial service, a funeral, or sitting Shiva for your infant, whether you choose to take your baby's remains or not. A funeral director can provide assistance as to what to do. A memorial service can be anywhere—your home, church, synagogue, hospital chapel, funeral chapel, or in a park. Your clergy will probably also have ideas about services or ceremonies for your baby. Such a service may not be customary in your religious community and you may have to make special arrangements.

Burial or cremation. If you want to explore options for burial, cremation, or funeral services, call a funeral director to check on your rights and options. The cost should be minimal, depending on your decisions and where you live. It is also a good idea to ask about the laws in your state governing the burial or disposition of a miscarried baby.

Pathology report. Your medical attendant might recommend testing the baby and the placenta at the time of miscarriage. You should be asked for your permission and may be required to sign a form if this testing is to be done. If it is, you have the right to know what the results are. The test results should be explained to you and your partner by your medical attendant. It often takes up to 6 weeks to get the pathology report back. If you are not contacted by your caregiver with the results of the tests, do not hesitate to call and inquire.

Chromosome-genetic studies. These studies are not to be confused with the pathology tests. Fetal chromosome studies are recommended because they may be able to detect the cause of the miscarriage. These studies might be possible only if the baby died close to the time of the miscarriage. As unsatisfactory as it might seem, often the tests cannot answer all of your questions about why this has happened to you. However, it might be able to rule out some potential risk factors for future pregnancies.

****

The options and decisions can feel overwhelming. You may choose all of the options mentioned above or only a few. Whatever you decide, remember that not all decisions are permanent. For example, even though you might choose not to name your baby now, there may come a day when you want to. It's not too late then.

You and your partner might not agree on all of the options and decisions you face. Try to talk through the options and do your best to minimize the potential regrets. Remember, you are making the best decisions you can at the time. Please yourself and don't worry about the rest of the world and what they will think of your decisions.

What causes miscarriage to happen?

After a miscarriage it is normal to wonder why this has happened. There are several possible reasons why miscarriages occur, although often the cause remains unknown. The inability to discover exactly what went wrong can be very frustrating. If you are lucky enough to find out the cause of your miscarriage, some of your frustration might be eased. Talk with your medical attendant about the following potential causes to determine if any might have caused your miscarriage.

Possible Causes

One thing is for certain: pregnancy cannot be wished away. Nor can it be ended by a minor fall. Miscarriages don't usually happen as a result of wearing high heel shoes, exercising, or by making love too often or vigorously. Nor are miscarriages brought on as a punishment from God for past misdeeds. Yet, often in your desire to figure out why, you may have considered explanations like these. The reality is that miscarriage is not fair! Yet miscarriages do happen. There is usually no logical or adequate explanation. Not having an explanation can sometimes make it more difficult to accept the miscarriage.

Causes or explanations of miscarriage are generally grouped according to these factors: *fetal, parental,* and *external. Fetal factors* are problems with the fetus and its development. *Parental factors* are problems in the mother or father that might cause miscarriage, such as disease or anatomical malformations. *External factors* are those things in the environment that might cause miscarriage.

Medical terms used to describe the causes of miscarriage can often sound judgmental. Terms such as "defective" sperm or "incompetent" cervix may hit you wrong, causing a reaction. Keep in mind that such descriptions are of a medical nature and are not descriptions of you or the performance of your body.

Fetal Factors

Chromosomal Abnormalities. Studies show that more than 50% of all first-trimester miscarriages are caused by chromosomal abnormalities, such as extra or missing genetic information, that prevent the fetus from developing normally. Chromosomal abnormalities may be inherited from a parent due to rearrangements in parental chromosomes. This results in an egg or sperm with an unbalanced genetic makeup. Most abnormalities, however, are due to random error in the chromosome distribution in the egg or sperm. In order to determine which is the case, chromosome studies must be specifically requested on the fetal tissue at the time of the miscarriage. Although these studies often are not successful, they should be attempted, if at all possible, because the information they can provide can be valuable.

Genetic studies on you and your partner might be suggested if fetal chromosome studies were not successful, if you have had two or more pregnancy losses, or if your family history indicates it.

Defective Implantation. What occurs in defective implantation is different than what takes place in an ectopic pregnancy. In defective implantation, the fertilized egg is in the uterus but is unable to implant in the uterine wall. Thus, the pregnancy cannot continue normally.

Faulty Fertilization. For some unexplained reason a problem with the fertilization process can occur, preventing the embryo from continuing normal development.

Placental Problems. Problems in the development or functioning of the placenta may prevent the fetus from getting adequate nourishment. Placental problems can also include problems with the umbilical cord.

Parental Factors

Defective Egg or Sperm. The egg or sperm that united to form the embryo may have been malformed or too old at the time of conception for continued development to occur.

Hormonal Imbalance. This most commonly involves a defect of the luteal phase of the menstrual cycle. The same types of hormonal problems that caused infertility may also cause miscarriage. Sometimes fertility drugs can contribute to these hormonal imbalances, resulting in miscarriage.

Infection. Infection in the mother might cause miscarriage in a number of different ways. Examples of diseases potentially dangerous to the fetus are syphilis, herpes simplex, and CMV (cytomegalovirus). Some bacterial infections that might cause miscarriage are pneumonia, urinary tract infection, bowel infection, or uterine infection. Some medical conditions that might cause miscarriage are thyroid disease, diabetes, heart disease, or hypertension. Viral infections potentially causing miscarriage are measles, hepatitis, polio, encephalitis, chickenpox, and toxoplasmosis.

A disease of pregnancy that can be fatal for the baby and cause serious health concerns for the mother is *toxemia.* The result of high blood pressure, it usually is not a problem early in pregnancy.

There is a higher risk of miscarriage among women who are younger than 18 and older than 35 years. There is also a higher risk in women who have diseases such as systemic lupus erythematosus, multiple sclerosis (MS), chlamydia trachomatis, and ureaplasma urealyticum (T-mycoplasma).

Immunological Factors. The incompatability of parental blood types can cause miscarriage, although this type of miscarriage usually occurs late in pregnancy.

Uterine Disorders. Malformations of the uterus may be congenital, such as those resulting from DES exposure, or they may result from a disease such as Asherman's syndrome.

Incompetent Cervix. In some women, the cervix is abnormally weak. This may be congenital or the result of obstetrical or surgical injury. Incompetent cervix is usually the cause of miscarriage later in pregnancy, as the baby becomes heavier and pressure on the cervix induces premature labor.

Sperm Problems. Miscarriage might sometimes occur as a result of a very high or very low sperm count, or as a result of poor sperm quality. Decreased DNA content in the sperm can also result in miscarriage. Certain diseases in the father, such as diabetes, can also contribute to miscarriage. The father's exposure to toxic substances such as Agent Orange have been linked to miscarriage and birth defects.

External Factors

Injury. Serious injury such as that caused by a car accident can cause miscarriage if it occurs during a critical point in fetal development.

Environmental Causes. Environmental pollutants have been linked to higher miscarriage rates. Examples include exposure to radiation, toxic waste, and herbicides such as Agent Orange. Cigarette smoking, poor nutrition, and drug abuse have also been linked to higher rates of miscarriage. Incidence of miscarriage is doubled in women who are moderate to heavy drinkers.

What are my chances of having another miscarriage?

Although this is a question that is very important to you, it is one that cannot easily be answered. One miscarriage is not necessarily a predictor of another. Many medical attendants believe that until three or more miscarriages have occured the chances of another pregnancy loss are not significantly increased. However, there is some statistical evidence that there may be a slightly increased risk of miscarriage in future pregnancies.

Age seems to be a factor that might affect the recurrence of miscarriage. There appears to be an increasing risk after the age of 35 years as well as under age 18.

Certain causes of miscarriage, such as luteal phase defect, previous infertility, or incompetent cervix, can result in an increased risk of miscarriage in subsequent pregnancies. Frequently, however, these conditions can be treated.

If the cause of your miscarriage can be determined and treated, the chances of another miscarriage are greatly reduced. You may be encouraged as a precaution by your medical attendant to abstain from sexual intercourse during the first trimester of the next pregnancy or you may be restricted to bedrest in an effort to ensure the continuation of the pregnancy. It is important to seek out medical attention that is supportive and knowledgeable in order to minimize your risk of another miscarriage.

What about habitual miscarriage?

The generally accepted definition of recurrent or habitual miscarriage is three or more consecutive losses. The causes of recurrent miscarriages are much the same as the causes of single miscarriages. The most common causes of habitual miscarriage are genetic problems, Rh incompatibility, incompetent cervix, hormonal imbalance, uterine defect, or illness in one or both of the parents. Some of these conditions can be treated, but, unfortunately, it may take more than one pregnancy loss to determine the problem and to establish correct treatment.

A major concern may be, what are your chances of a successful pregnancy? In making a decision about another pregnancy or gearing up emotionally to handle another pregnancy, it can be helpful to know what the odds are. Sadly, there are very few accurate statistics on the incidence of miscarriage in subsequent pregnancy and those that exist may not apply to your specific situation.

As a result, the psychological toll of one miscarriage after another can be great. It is common to regrieve past miscarriages and previous losses at the same time as the present miscarriage. This might seem overwhelming to you or your partner. It is a reaction of recurrent miscarriage that should not be underestimated.

Some people find subsequent miscarriages to be less threatening and devastating than their first, perhaps because they have been through it before and know what to expect. It's important to talk this out with your partner, since you may or may not be on the same wavelength. It is also important to recognize that each miscarriage can have a different effect and bring forth a variety of feelings. One miscarriage might have been felt only mildly, while another can seem a catastrophe.

Talk about your concerns and the differences in each loss. Try not to let yourself be overcome by the many losses. Yet, do remember, that you are suffering more than just this present miscarriage. In addition, be certain to obtain expert medical care from a specialist in high-risk pregnancy.

After infertility, why did I miscarry?

The incidence of miscarriage following infertility is increased for a number of reasons. The condition that caused your infertility, such as poor sperm quality, uterine tumors, or a luteal phase defect, may have contributed to your miscarriage. Or the treatment itself, including ovulation-inducing drugs (eg, Clomid and Pergonal) or in vitro fertilization, may have been a factor in your miscarriage.

If you experience a miscarriage after struggling with infertility, you might find your emotional reaction one of extreme despair. Even before your miscarriage your excitement and happiness about the pregnancy may have been mingled with fear and anxiety. Such a reaction is a normal response to months or even years of emotional investment in the child you so wanted to have. This may be especially true if you feel this was your only chance to have a child. Miscarriage can be a cruel blow, unfair and unreal, especially when pregnancy has been such a longstanding and important goal in your life.

Infertility can take a toll on your self-esteem, your partnership, and other relationships. The roller coaster of hopes raised and hopes dashed month after month can be grueling. You might feel out of control, out of synch with your peers, and overwhelmed. Often the medical treatment needed to restore your fertility can feel demeaning and uncomfortable. If your feelings seem overwhelming, it may be that you are reacting to the combined loss of your fertility and your pregnancy.

It is important to get emotional support and the medical care necessary in order to minimize the potential stress. You may want to seek out a urologist or gynecologist who specializes in infertility. Many couples have received a great deal of support from contact with others who have experienced infertility and miscarriage (see RESOURCES pages 50-51).

What happens to my body after a miscarriage?

A woman's body goes through a number of physical and emotional changes in the process of returning to normal after a miscarriage. This process can take weeks and even months. Some women report that, although they were menstruating, they did not feel "normal" for several months following their miscarriage. Due to hormonal changes you may find that it takes longer than you anticipated to get a menstrual period. You may experience emotional mood swings, find that you cry more easily and more often than is normal for you, are more irritable, or tire more easily. Eventually, the fullness in the abdomen and breasts subsides, nausea ceases, and the uterus contracts down to its normal size.

Breasts may continue to be tender and full for some time. Some women even experience their milk coming in after a miscarriage. If this is the case for you, you might find binding your breasts helpful. The normal feelings of loss and emptiness: can be compounded by the breast tenderness and milk "let down."

It is important not to postpone or overlook the follow-up exam with your medical attendant, which is usually done four to six weeks after your miscarriage. Your partner may wish to attend this exam with you to discuss such concerns as expectations and timing of future pregnancies, when to resume sexual intercourse, the impact of this miscarriage on your health or fertility, and feelings that may be troubling either of you. At this time the results of any lab tests that were done might be available. Chromosome studies probably would not be complete yet.

Following a miscarriage, it is usually recommended that you use sanitary napkins rather than tampons and that you do not have sexual intercourse until the bleeding has stopped.

If you experience any of the following warning signs you should contact your medical attendant immediately. Don't wait until your scheduled appointment if you have:

—vaginal bleeding that increases significantly or persists over several weeks' time
—a fever of 100° or over
—bleeding that changes to bright red
—pelvic pain or unusual cramping
—discharge that has a bad odor or is infected-looking (yellow or green)

Any of these symptoms could indicate an infection or retained tissue and should be treated immediately.

3

Coping: Taking Care Of Yourself

Nuture strength of spirit
*   to shield you in sudden misfortune.*
But do not distress yourself with imaginings.
Many fears are born of fatigue and loneliness.
Beyond a wholesome discipline,
Be gentle with yourself.
*   Desiderata*

After a miscarriage you might understand your feelings, yet have a difficult time coping with them. This is normal. A miscarriage is a life event that has the potential to upset your equilibrium. There are many areas of your life to keep in balance: physical, mental, social, emotional, and spiritual.

Having to cope with many changes in a short time—pregnancy, miscarriage, and medical treatment—can make you more vulnerable to illness and disease. Balancing your needs and the stressors in your life isn't an easy task.

Coping, which can be either active or passive, helps you keep your balance. Active coping is taking charge of the situation in order to reduce stress. Passive coping is being able to identify and accept the unchangeable. Because our culture equates coping with doing something, passive coping can be more difficult for many.

Although active coping is more commonly used to decrease stress, passive coping is needed too. Active coping can help you change the direction of things while passive coping can help you accept your loss and let go of it. Combining both kinds of coping can make the path of adjustment smoother for you. The following suggestions might help give you ideas about how to cope with your miscarriage. This list include both active and passive coping methods. Keep in mind that these suggestions apply to both partners.

Allow yourself to grieve if grief is what you feel. Grief is a mixture of feelings: sadness, disappointment, anger, bewilderment, shock, denial, and depression. It is a process through which you move in an unstructured manner. Although there is a fairly common pattern to grief, each person grieves uniquely.

You might fear the tears and sadness of grief, believing that if you allow some of your feelings out, you will be overwhelmed by them. Actually, this is not often the case. If you keep your feelings bottled up it can prevent you from getting over your miscarriage and moving on. Pent-up feelings also have the potential of growing stronger and more destructive with time. Look for the books listed under Grief in the Bibliography.

Exercise. A brisk walk can be helpful for many reasons: a change of scenery, some activity, and a chance to be in the fresh air. Exercise need not be vigorous—it can be any kind of physical activity you have found pleasurable in the past.

Cut down or eliminate use of tobacco, alcohol, or chemicals. Although now is not the time to change potentially harmful habits, it is a good idea to try to rely on them less often. Alcohol, marijuana, and tranquilizing drugs are depressants that can work against the progress you are trying to make.

Eat well. Do not go on a reducing diet at this time, even though you might wish to lose the weight you gained during your pregnancy. What you need is a well-balanced diet high in bulk, protein, and vitamins. If you have been the kind of person who turns to food as a source of comfort, try to cut down or eliminate junk food and do not skip meals. It is also a good idea to drink lots of water and fruit juices.

Keep a journal. You might find that keeping a journal of your feelings, thoughts, and memories will help you work through your grief or sadness. Some parents write letters to their babies, sharing feelings they never had the chance to express.

Talk with others who have had similar experiences. You may have the opportunity to talk about your feelings in either a formal or informal setting. You may choose to join a support group or contact a parent-to-parent reachout program. Or you may choose to talk with friends, family, or others who have had miscarriages. This can help you feel less isolated, less alone, and less unique in your loss.

Read books and literature on the subject. Some people need to understand intellectually what has happened before they can understand it emotionally. Reading can be an important aid in gaining this understanding. It can also provide comfort, information, and guidance.

Communicate with your partner, family, and friends. Talking about your feelings can be a valuable means of gaining comfort and understanding. Some people need to "talk out" their feelings in order to understand them. In the process of talking they gain additional insight. Others need to sort the experience out alone before they can discuss it with others. This is an important difference for you and your partner to recognize. Don't be surprised if the two of you express your feelings in different ways and at different times.

Lower your expectations of yourself. Determine what must be done, and then let yourself off the hook for the rest. You might not be able to do as much as you did before, but you will reach that level again sometime in the near future. Remember that you will find your "new normal" soon. Right now you are probably doing your grief work, which is important and can be time-consuming.

Avoid making major decisions. Decisions about sterilization, immediate pregnancy, major career plans, or a move should be postponed, if possible, until you can give them your full attention.

Meditation and visualization. Meditation can be a helpful method of giving you some reprieve from your grief work. Visualization or imaging is a form of self-hypnosis in which one imagines a calm, comforting setting and journeys there in their imagination. There are several books and tapes available on this very helpful relaxation technique.

Force yourself to concentrate on one thing at a time, one day at a time. Don't let yourself become overwhelmed by all the things you need to do or minor details. Try to concentrate on the task at hand, one thing at a time.

Try to find comfort in nature. Nature can be a valuable resource: spring comes, flowers bloom again, winter doesn't last forever. Spending time outdoors and observing nature can provide hope and faith in life and its continuing cycles of renewal.

Get enough sleep. Not being well rested can have a detrimental effect on your emotional and physical well-being. However, getting enough sleep can be difficult, especially in the days just following a miscarriage. Some suggestions to keep in mind to help in getting a good night's sleep are: try not to discuss upsetting subjects late in the evening; cut out caffeine-containing beverages after dinner; try not to go to bed angry; reduce physical and mental activity at least a half hour before going to bed; and don't go to bed before you are tired. You might also try taking a hot bath or drinking a glass of warm milk before going to bed.

Massage. Many couples find that a massage or backrub is very calming and also allows them a quiet time together in which they can relax and talk. This is also a good way to give each other undivided attention.

Positive self talk. Be careful of making this event bigger that it really is. If you find yourself saying, "Because of this my life will never be happy again," bring yourself back. You CAN be happy again. There are things in life that probably can make you happy even now, although you may have temporarily lost sight of them. You might want to read more about this in *Feeling Good: The New Mood Therapy* by David Burns, MD.

Pay attention to unnecessary "shoulds" you might tell yourself. Sometimes the "stiff upper lip" approach can lead to unrealistic demands on yourself, such as "I should be over this by now" or "I really should go to this baby shower even though the thought of it makes me miserable." Recognize your limitations and needs. Don't force yourself to do something that makes you uncomfortable, and don't put any time limit on your recovery.

Develop or utilize your spirituality. Many have found support not only in their religious beliefs, but in the community of people who share those beliefs. You may have more in common with your religious community than you realize and find more comfort than you expect.

Try to use God and your faith as a source of comfort, not a source or "cause" of this misfortune. You are not the first to ask "why" of God. You might want to read *When Bad Things Happen to Good People* by Harold Kushner.

****

Healing and recovery is a process. It is a process that takes time. Although time is no guarantee of recovery, don't be impatient with yourself if it takes longer than you anticipated. Try to determine what works for you and be kind to yourself.

4

The Days Ahead: Different Reactions

The family is the nucleus of civilization.
Will and Ariel Durant

When a birth or death occurs in a family, each member experiences a change and reacts to it. Miscarriage, a unique event in the life of a family, is both a birth and a death, a beginning and an ending. It's a time of adjustment as the family rearranges itself and deals with the loss of an expected member.

Each family member's response to the miscarriage depends upon such things as how the other family members felt about the pregnancy; how the family traditionally deals with change, crisis, and death; other losses the family may have experienced in the past; resources available to them; and the community's interpretation of the miscarriage.

In order to understand your own and your family's reaction to your miscarriage, it might be helpful to understand a little about families and how they operate. The behaviors of one member cause a reaction in the others. Family members' reactions tend to balance each other out, providing some sense of security and predictability. Often family members can be great sources of strength to each other, providing support and comfort during trying times. However, this is not always true.

A family that is basically healthy does some of the following: communicates and listens; respects and trusts each other; has a sense of humor and playfulness; shares and uses spirituality as strength; shares leisure time; and admits to and seeks help when problems develop. You can read more about this in Dolores Curran's book, *Traits of a Healthy Family*.

The manner in which you and your family adjust to the changes following your

25

miscarriage depends not only on how your family handles crisis and change, but on other things that may be going on in your lives. The existence of other stressful events is something you might overlook as you strive to deal with this experience. There may be any number of things happening in your life: a job change, a move, unemployment, marital conflict, a sick family member, or a normal transition, such as a preschooler starting kindergarten. In addition, previous losses. especially other pregnancy losses, are likely to influence how you cope now. You might find yourself or your family regrieving those losses or you might find those experiences actually make this one easier.

By looking at your family, your previous losses, your current lifestyle, and the investment you and family members had in this pregnancy, you can probably better understand why each of you is reacting in a unique way.

Women

A Prayer for Baby

Never to have known you, but to have loved you.
Never to have held you, the way mothers do.

With you I bury my hopes and dreams
For an unknown child I'd never seen.

But also I bury the love in my heart
And the sadness of knowing that we must part.

And I pray to God to do for you
All the things that I would like to do.

And to keep my baby safe from harm
To laugh and frolic in springtime's arms.

Anonymous

Your reaction to your miscarriage is unique and different from that of other family members. You were pregnant, carrying this unborn child, and most likely you experienced some physical signs or symptoms of pregnancy. You were sharing your body with your baby and now you are not. Therefore, you probably feel not only the loss of your child, but the loss of part of yourself as well. You might grieve for the baby you wished to give birth to and for the loss of your future with this child. Perhaps the end of the excitement of being pregnant is the greater loss for you. In certain circumstances, you may be mourning the loss of your fertility and the opportunity to experience another pregnancy. Another possible trauma could be the medical treatment or life threatening circumstances surrounding your miscarriage.

Whatever your situation, it is important to understand that any of these concerns and losses are likely to influence your feelings about your miscarriage. Whatever is the greater loss for you, try to accept rather than criticize or discount your feelings, even when they may be conflicting.

Talking about your miscarriage is one way of making sense of it and getting through it. However, you might be the kind of woman who needs to sort things out within yourself before you can discuss your experience with others. It is important to recognize what kind of person you are and give yourself the right environment for taking care of yourself. If you need to be alone for awhile, tell that to those around you. If you need to talk, find someone you feel comfortable with and sound off.

A miscarriage brings two endings: the end of your baby's life and the end of your pregnancy. The end of pregnancy often brings emotional changes as well as physical ones. It is often difficult to determine where your feelings are coming from—your grief or your hormones! Understanding this may make it easier for you to accept the mood swings, sudden crying spells, fatigue, or irritability you might experience. Don't expect too much of yourself, even though a surge in energy following a miscarriage is sometimes common. The return to routine activities should be slow and gradual, depending on your physical and emotional health.

Sexual activity after a miscarriage can sometimes be a sensitive issue. You might be disinterested or even want to avoid sexual intercourse because it reminds you of how your baby's life began or it could be physically uncomfortable. On the other hand, you might desire the comfort and closeness of sexual intimacy especially at this time. Keep in mind that you can be loving without having intercourse. Talk with your partner about feelings and needs. Allow yourself time for working things out and for being sexually close.

Finally, take care of yourself. If you are a mother with other children at home, you might find yourself so busy caring for them that you lose track of yourself and your own needs. Or if you are a mother working outside the home, you might discover that while your work is a welcome outlet, you may have too many irons in the fire. Its common to expect too much of yourself to soon. Try not to allow yourself to become over tired and emotionally drained.

Men

Everything we have done has been faithful and dangerous
We believed in the promises made by the brows of women.
We begot children at night in the warm wool.
We comforted those who wept in fear on our shoulders.
Those who comforted us had themselves vanished.
Archibald MacLeish

During and after the miscarriage you, the father, might find yourself confronted by a flood of emotions and concerns. Perhaps you did not have enough time to realize or believe in the reality of the baby when the miscarriage occurred. This is a very common reaction. Studies have shown that men "bond" to a pregnancy differently than their partners. Usually the father lags behind the mother anywhere from a few weeks to a trimester in emotional attachment to the baby.

You might find yourself concerned about the baby, but even more concerned about your partner's health and well-being. This is especially true if her condition was an emergency requiring immediate medical attention. Perhaps you felt intimidated by medical institutions or staff, which added to your feeling of confusion and helplessness.

You could respond to the miscarriage in any number of ways. You might feel disappointed but not necessarily distraught, or you could feel resigned and accepting. You may feel angry or frustrated, wanting to lash out at something or someone. Another common reaction you might have is confusion about your feelings. It's possible that you might feel uncomfortable about asking questions or asking for assistance. Concern about future pregnancies or the ability to have a family are other things you might have on your mind.

You may find medical attendants, family members, or clergy expecting you to take care of your partner. Your partner may even expect you to be supportive of her and not concerned or upset yourself. Although that role might be important and acceptable to you, don't lose sight of your own emotional needs. After all, you were the expectant father and have a responsibility to acknowledge those feelings.

It can be very difficult to express your feelings when the people around you expect you not to. Don't let this discourage you; do what you need to do. Discuss your feelings with your partner or seek out a friend or family member who can listen and be there for you. Remember that sharing your feelings can also build or strengthen your bond with your partner. Furthermore, sharing feelings prevents those around you from guessing—often incorrectly—how you really feel.

Being "required" to be strong is different than choosing to be. If you feel disappointed and hurt about this miscarriage, being strong can be very lonely and isolating. Being able to share these feelings with your partner can be very valuable for both of you as you learn that being strong can be something you take turns at and is not the responsibility of just one partner.

Perhaps you think that becoming involved in your work or other activities is best for you and everyone else. Sharing your feelings about the miscarriage may be especially difficult if your partner is very upset. As one man said, "I felt like if I said I was sad, life would just become endless tears—hers, mine, and ours—and it would never end." It may seem that turning to your work may be the only comfort and distraction you have.

Many men do have a hard time talking about personal unhappiness and find they have few opportunities to do so. A support group, either for men or for couples, can give you a chance to talk. You may discover, as many other men have, that talking about your feelings makes them less frightening and overwhelming.

One of the more difficult feelings you may experience after a miscarriage is anger. This feeling can be confusing to you because the anger may be vented at everyone: your partner, the medical attendants, the clergy, God, or even yourself. Sometimes your anger may remain unspoken, seething but felt by those around you. Anger itself is not bad, but it can be very destructive when it is allowed to smolder or when it erupts uncontrollably.

You may find that a physical activity such as chopping wood, running, or hitting tennis balls provides a release for your angry feelings. Or it might be helpful to talk about what it is that makes you angry: the unfairness of it all, the manner in which your wife was treated, or how you were overlooked. Anger can be a great impetus for action, motivating you to make changes in your personal life, the medical community, or the community at large.

Anger at ourselves or others is known as blame. You may blame yourself for the miscarriage, wondering whether you had been a better provider or partner the miscarriage might have been prevented. Maybe you wondered if your partner did anything to cause the miscarriage. Or both of you may have blamed sex, wondering if having intercourse may have caused the miscarriage.

Even though blame is an attempt to make sense of what has happened, it is usually an unproductive attempt. In some cases, placing blame might be helpful, but usually it leaves you with no more answers and may even create emotional pain for your or rifts between you and those you love. It is important to remember that the events cannot be altered, the miscarriage cannot be reversed, and blame is of little use now.

After a miscarriage there can be a lot of things to think about: your partner, medical bills, the future and other pregnancies, your children, and your work, to mention only a few. You may find that you have so many things on your mind that you are easily distracted, unable to concentrate on what you are doing or to remember things. If your powers of concentration are not normal, avoid using heavy machinery, driving, or doing other activities that might be dangerous.

Some men are surprised by crying spells in the car, when they are alone or at odd times. Do not be alarmed by this, it is only natural. With time you will return to a normal level of functioning. Trust yourself and use these changes in behavior as signals of what you need—whether it is time to talk, think, relax; time to be alone; or time to be with your partner and family.

As the expectant father, you too had hopes and dreams. You too had a shattered promise. You can give yourself and your partner a precious gift: talk about your loss, communicate openly, and take care of yourself.

Couples

Now I do believe
That even in the storm
We'll find some light.
Knowing you're beside me
I'm alright.
          Marvin Hamlisch

At the time of your miscarriage and afterwards, each of you will react in your own way. This is due to differences in personality style, beliefs about expressing feelings and pain, previous experiences, and family background. You might find yourselves grieving immediately or it might take longer for what has happened to really hit you.

In the beginning one of you might feel very sad, while the other seems unaffected or angry. Partners often take turns taking care of each other and being supportive. One of you might be outwardly grieving while the other is providing support and understanding. Later these roles may reverse. This is one of the strengths of families that helps them work during stressful times.

Sometimes, however, these opposite coping styles can cause conflict between the two of you. Maybe you feel that your partner doesn't care or is unconcerned. Or perhaps you are anxious to move on from the loss and feel upset by your partner's inability to do so. This conflict may be the result of an unrealistic belief in an ideal relationship, one in which you both feel the same, grieve the same, and recover at the same pace. After a loss, it can be disappointing to realize that you each have unique needs and coping strategies. If you are having difficulty supporting each other through this loss, try not to blame each other or be discouraged about your relationship. Grief is a singular process. Each of you will move through the healing process in your own way. Knowing this can take the pressure off both of you.

Communication might become strained after your miscarriage. This could be a problem that existed before the miscarriage, or it might be an aftermath of the miscarriage. It isn't always easy to share true feelings with one another. Real problems can arise when concerns are not discussed and become hiding places for unspoken feelings and resentments. It is difficult to keep a relationship flowering and healthy without the life-giving rain that communication provides.

If you cannot work out your communication problems on your own, seek out a person who can help you, such as a clergy person, counselor, or family physician. You might want to consider different ways to work on good communication, such as marriage encounter sessions, support groups, talking with others who have had similar experiences, or additional time just with each other.

Sometimes there are differences of opinion about issues relating to the miscarriage, such as when to try to have another baby or when to resume sexual intercourse. It is difficult to resolve these conflicts if they are not talked about or if you lack the information necessary to make such decisions. Do your best to educate yourself about the decisions you face. This can be done by reading, talking with your medical attendant, or by contacting resource organizations (see RESOURCES pages 47-48). Finally, talking together about the issues will help you through the process of decision-making.

Take care of your relationship. Treat yourselves to a night out every so often, go for walks together, give each other back rubs, or write "love notes" to each other that will be found in unexpected places. Give each other your love, an accepting attitude, and your comforting assurance that you are there when and if you are needed. You may have lost your baby but you still have each other.

Single Women

The joys of parents are secret,
And so are their griefs and fears.
Francis Bacon

As a single woman, whether you have a steady partner or not, you may feel alone, isolated, or misunderstood. Friends, family, and even medical professionals might assume that you are pleased or at least relieved about your miscarriage whether or not this is the case. If you have strong feelings of disappointment you might find little support from those who think "it's for the best."

Sometimes it's difficult to share your loss with family members. The miscarriage might create complications in your relationships with your family or other children. Trying to keep thoughts and feelings private can be an additional burden. Difficulty may stem from sharing the miscarriage with those who want to chastise you for the pregnancy rather than comfort you for the loss. Single motherhood is not generally accepted in our culture, even today. Therefore, a single woman's pregnancy loss is even less likely to be understood and recognized. This can result in a lack of support and compassion from those around you.

Your reactions to the miscarriage might range from feelings of guilt or shame to extreme disappointment at the loss of the child, your potential companion. You might be relieved yet sad at the same time.

Perhaps the baby was your only link with the baby's father and the end of the pregnancy means the loss of him as well as the baby. Or the miscarriage may have resulted in a closer relationship with your partner, as sharing this experience made his commitment to you more obvious.

Additional burdens that you might face are financial insecurity and concerns about your health. Medical and emotional assistance might be available through your county or other helping agencies. Don't hesitate to discuss these concerns with your caregiver.

Sorting out your feelings about the miscarriage may also entail sorting out your feelings about other people and the relationships in your life. A support group or private counseling might prove to be valuable in helping you find your way through your confusion. It can also help you discover how much you have in common with other women, whether married or not, who have suffered a miscarriage. Remember that no matter what your situation or feelings about the loss, you should be kind to yourself and take good care of your body and soul.

Siblings

We Are Seven

A simple child,
That light draws its breath,
And feels its life in every limb,
What should it know of death?

I met a little cottage girl:
She was eight years old, she said;
Her hair was thick with many a curl
That clustered round her head.

"Sisters and brothers, little maid,
How many may you be?"
"How many? Seven in all," she said,
And wondering looked at me.

"How many are you, then" said I,
"If they two are in heaven?"
Quick was the little maid's reply:
"O Master! we are seven."

"But they are dead; those two are dead!
Their spirits are in heaven!"-
'T was throwing words away; for still
The little maid would have her will,
And said, "Nay, we are seven!"

William Wordsworth

If you have other children you might wonder if you should talk with them about the miscarriage. Do they know what is going on and should you tell them about it at all? As a rule, it is not a good idea to keep a miscarriage or any similar event a secret from children. This is especially true if the children have been told about the pregnancy. By sharing family events and seeing you deal with them, your children can learn about life and how to deal with the challenges life presents. Furthermore, children frequently sense such things and may have more knowledge of what has happened than you suspect. Being left alone to make sense of events and information (whether it is correct or not) can have a more harmful effect on your child than the truth itself.

Even very young children understand the concepts of pregnancy, babies, and death. This can be seen in the drawing below by a four-year-old boy. He explained, "The mommy dinosaur is sad and crying because the baby dinosaur inside her has died. Her other boy is watching. He is sad, too."

TOMON

When explaining your miscarriage, try to adapt your explanation to your child's age and intellectual capacity. Also keep in mind your child's personality and temperament, because these will offer you clues on how your child is understanding and coping with the loss. It might be helpful to relate this experience to previous experiences your child may have had with death, such as the death of a grandparent or pet.

Do not think that you have not explained everything adequately if your child continues to ask questions like, "Where is the baby?" "Is the baby still in your tummy?" Children need to make the experience real by going over the same information again and again. It's likely that your child will ask a lot of questions and want to talk about this event for some time. Children, like adults, need time and information to sort out this type of event and incorporate it into their experience.

Children's understanding of pregnancy, birth, and death differs with their age. The differences in their understanding and reaction are summarized in the chart below.

Age	Understanding and Response
0 to 6 months	No concept of death; no verbalization skills; may respond to parent's grief, especially that of primary caregiver.
6 to 18 months	Earliest concept of death; believe it is a temporary separation or absence; respond to parental grief.
18 months to 5 years	Understand death as an altered and permanent state but still have difficulty comprehending; fear for own safety; may experience confusion or guilt as a result of ambivalent feelings about awaited sibling; magical thinking: believe they could have done something to cause the miscarriage, perhaps by wishing it away, and can solve it by wishing the baby back.
5 to 8 years	Understand death is a natural process and that death could happen to them; magical thinking: they could have caused or prevented the miscarriage; typical for child to appear unaffected yet inwardly feel very upset; attempt to control feelings like a grown-up.
8 to 12 years	Adult concept of death; may become concerned for their own life as they become aware of "randomness" of death; may be more concerned for mother's health than with death of the baby; may be more concerned about their own or their parent's death.
Adolescent	Adult concept of death; reaction may be mingled with confused feelings about their own sexuality and obvious sexuality of parents who have created the baby; may experience profound grief as a result of being able to bond to awaited sibling on more adult level.

You might feel so upset and troubled by your miscarriage that your grief or medical needs interrupt your homelife. Your surviving children may feel they have lost not only a potential "playmate" and sibling but also you, their parent(s), in the bargain. They might feel alone, unable to talk with others about the loss, or feel guilty for finding enjoyment in play and regular activities. Yet it's important to remember that although you want to help your children, you might not be able to be the perfect parent. Remember, you may have to meet your own needs first.

Keep in mind that you will not be able to handle everything perfectly at all times. You should not expect that and neither should your children. Don't feel guilty; just try to do your best and give your children your love. If your child has a marked behavior change and you are not in an emotional state to help, do not hesitate to reach out to family, friends, or professionals in your community for some assistance.

In discussing the miscarriage with your children keep in mind some of these suggestions:

Listen to your child. Give him or her your acceptance.This will enable your child to share concerns and questions with you.

Be honest with your child. Don't avoid explanations. Be factual and honest. If you don't know, say so, eg, "I don't know why babies die before they are born; it confuses me too." If you can find the answer to your child's questions, try to do so.

Accept your child's feelings. Let your child talk about anger, hurt, sadness, concerns for mom and her health, or whatever he or she is worried about.

Give your child brief explanations. Try to be concise in answering your child's questions; don't give lengthy answers beyond his or her comprehension or interest.

Show your love and warmth. Hold, rock, sing, and spend special time with your child. Each child needs the reassurance that the special place they have held in your heart is still there even though you mourn another child.

Share your own feelings and encourage your child to do the same. It can be difficult to talk with your child about painful and unhappy feelings, but by doing so you give permission to your child to share his or her feelings and provide a model for doing so.

Allow yourself to cry in front of your child.

Be patient with yourself and your child.

Use examples in nature to explain death. Your child can be helped to understand death when it is related to the death of a pet, animal, or plant. A child may not understand when a dead mouse or bird is thrown into the garbage, for example. He or she may wonder if this is what was done with the baby, or would be done with him or her or other loved ones. Ceremonies such as funerals, cremations,or burials can help your child gain understanding of death as well as respect for life.

Allow your child to help with decisions. Seeing the baby or being involved with a memorial service might be a joint decision depending on the age of the child. This is especially important for the older child. Ask what he or she wants to do, yet give enough information so that your child can be prepared for what is happening.

Read to your children. Books can be an excellent way to share time and ideas with your children. They can help you begin discussions about topics like death that you may have a difficult time talking about. (See RESOURCES, pages 47-48).

Try to maintain some household routine. Don't send a very young child away from their home. A better solution might be to have a relative, friend, or babysitter come in and stay at your home. Try to set aside some time during the day when you can give your child undivided attention.

Encourage your child to draw pictures or tell or write stories. This can be a very important way to keep in touch with young imaginations, thoughts, and feelings, as well as a way of providing a release of these feelings for the child.

****

It is not a good idea to tell children that the baby is sleeping, "lost," or has been such a good baby that God has taken him or her away to live with Him. Nor should children be told that the baby went to the hospital to die or that the baby died inside mom without also telling the child that the baby has come out of mom and how. These explanations can lead to misunderstandings, confusion, and unnecessary fears or anger.

Finally, communicate with your children and be yourself—it is the best gift you can give them.

Grandparents

In Memory of My Dear Grandchild Anne Bradstreet
Who Deceased June 20, 1669
With troubled heart and trembling hand I write,
The heavens have changed to sorrow my delight.
How oft with disappointment have I met,
When I on fading things my hopes have set?
I knew she was but as a withering flower,
That's here today, perhaps gone in an hour;
Like as a bubble, or the brittle glass,
Or like a shadow turning as it was,
Farewell dear child, thou ne'er shall come to me,
But yet a while, and I shall go to thee,

Anne Bradstreet

It is common after a miscarriage to look to your own mother and father or other family members for support and comfort. This can be an invaluable source of help as you share together your disappointment, sadness, and the dreams that can no longer come true. You may even feel a renewed sense of family belonging. Parents usually have learned a great deal about life, death, and birth and it can be comforting for all of you to share what they have learned.

You may find, however, that for whatever reasons, your parents may not be the source of support you expected. Perhaps your relationship with each other was strained or not one of mutual support before the loss occurred. Maybe your parents do not see the miscarried child as a real baby or a real loss. Some grandparents feel a double sense of pain and disappointment at the loss of their grandchild and their inability to help you, their own child. They might be overwhelmed by your pain and wish to protect you from sadness and sorrow.

This loss also affects their lives and their dreams. The miscarried grandchild might have had special meaning to your parents. They may offer you advice or instruction as their way of providing support, but this may seem like they are trying to take over for you rather than support you. As a result of these and other factors, your parents might not be able to comfort you and may, in some cases, make coping with the miscarriage more difficult. It is important to keep this in mind and not to expect more from them than they can give.

If you have had a troubled relationship with your parents in the past, you may experience a renewed discomfort during this stressful time. Your miscarriage combined with the lack of a satisfying relationship with your parents can feel like a double loss.

Remember, too, they grew up in a different environment and in an era where miscarriages and losses were more common. Death was not usually openly discussed. Your parents might have a hard time understanding why you can't "put it away" and move on, if that is how they think you should handle it. You might try educating your parents about miscarriage and its meaning to you. On the other hand, it might be draining to undertake this shortly after your miscarriage. Sometimes sharing books such as this one or others listed in the RESOURCES (pages 47-48) can be helpful to family and friends in understanding what you are experiencing and what you need.

If your relationship with your parents has been a positive one, you may find your parents able to comfort you as no one else can. Their assistance, support, and caring can give you special understanding. And it may even provide a renewed sense of family belonging that helps compensate for your loss.

Whatever your interaction with your parents, however, there are ties that link you together. You share a common history and relationships. Even if you are unable or unwilling to accept the majority of your parents' beliefs or values, you can choose something about them that you do value and leave the rest behind. This can help minimize this loss for you and help you better understand each other.

Other Family and Friends

A faithful friend is the medicine of life.

After a miscarriage, you will probably find that some people are very understanding and comforting, while others feel awkward and uneasy around you. Some people might offer to share their personal experience with you. If it is an experience you can relate to, this might be helpful. But if it is one that says very loudly, "I had it worse than you," it might leave you feeling more needy. Some people may give you advice such as "Get pregnant again soon" or "It could have been worse if the baby were older." Others might expect that after a certain amount of time, you "should" be over it. After a few such reactions you may feel you don't know who can give you the support and understanding you need.

It is natural for people to feel uncomfortable and not know what to say to you or how to be helpful. Have patience with them. Most people do not mean to be unkind. In their attempts to say the right thing they might offend or hurt you. You will probably need to let them know what is appropriate for you and what is not.

Everyone copes differently and has unique beliefs about handling stress and family crisis. Not everyone is able to openly communicate in an accepting manner, even though they might try. Some people cannot be supportive to you because death or loss is a taboo subject for them, not to be talked about. Others might believe that someone or something must be blamed. Some people believe that sharing personal feelings is not healthy or helpful. They may be unable or unwilling to share or listen to the intimate feelings that can build or maintain closeness.

Some of your feelings and reactions could be a response to other people's coping styles. It is best to seek out someone who you can talk with in an accepting and nonjudgmental environment. Spend less time trying to get support from those who cannot, for whatever reasons, give it. Reach out to those who you know can be helpful and who care about you. Often support, understanding, and kindness comes from places you would least expect. If you are fortunate you will find some people who are both sensitive and able to be there for you.

****

Each family member reacts differently after a major life event like miscarriage. It is difficult to predict the reactions of yourself or others at such times. Try not to expect your family members to behave in any certain way. At the same time allow yourself to respond in your own unique way. Given the freedom to respond as needed, all family members can move through this experience more comfortably.

5

What About the Future?

What lies behind us
And what lies before us
Are tiny matters compared to
What lies within us.
Ralph Waldo Emerson

You might already be asking yourself "What now? What about another pregnancy?," especially if you want more children. You might be anxious to get pregnant again as soon as possible, or you might not be ready, either physically or emotionally, to deal with another pregnancy at this time. It's also possible that, due to medical conditions or other circumstances, you will have little or no chance for another pregnancy. Every situation is unique and you will have to look at both physical and emotional issues as you consider your options in the upcoming months and years.

As you struggle with your decisions, try to maintain open communication with your partner and medical caregiver; seek as much information and support as you can; and look within yourself to determine how emotionally and physically ready you are for whatever the future will hold. When considering the decision about another pregnancy, adoption, or no more children, it is a good idea to weigh all of the options carefully and become fully informed.

For you another pregnancy might not be an option or possibility. This might be because you are now or have been infertile or because you had medical complications after the miscarriage. If this miscarriage was one of several you might decide that the chances of emotional and physical pain with another pregnancy are too great. Perhaps another pregnancy is simply impossible because of your age or physical health.

Consider getting a second opinion when in doubt.

Whatever your situation you do have choices and alternatives. One option might be more attractive than others and none of them may seem as attractive as having a baby of your own, created in the "normal" way. A discussion of alternatives follows.

There are several books available that can provide valuable information. Do not hesitate to contact resources in your community such as DES Awareness, the March of Dimes, RESOLVE, and pregnancy loss support groups. Such organizations specialize in providing information to the public and can offer support as well.

Genetic Counseling

Knowledge is of two kinds.
We know a subject ourselves,
or we know where we can find
information upon it.
Dr. Samuel Johnson
1709-1784

Genetic counseling can sometimes be helpful in not only determining the cause of the miscarriage, but the risk to future pregnancies. It can provide some of the information you need to make decisions about future pregnancies. You can ask your medical attendant, local university, hospital, or perinatal center to help you find a genetic counselor in your area. A genetic counselor may not be able to answer all of your questions, but should be able to increase your understanding of any genetic problems that exist. In addition, your counselor can recommend or provide you with additional materials that may be helpful.

Subsequent Pregnancy

Second Sowing

For whom
The milk ungiven in the breast
When the child is gone?

For whom
The love locked up in the heart
That is left alone?

That golden yield
Split sod once, overflowed an August field,
Threshed out in pain upon September's floor,
Now hoarded high in barns, a sterile store.

Break down the bolted door;
Rip open, spread and pour
The grain upon the barren ground
Wherever crack in clod is found.

There is no harvest for the heart alone;
The seed of love must be
Eternally
Resown

Anne Morrow Lindbergh

Readiness for another pregnancy depends on a number of different factors: your physical health, both your and your partner's emotional recovery, and the stability of your relationship, to name a few. You might be anxious about making a commitment to another pregnancy, to dare to hope and love again. This is natural. Yet if your next pregnancy results in the birth of a healthy baby, your feelings about your previous loss(es) may become more tolerable.

After a miscarriage, it is not unusual to feel apprehension or dread about another pregnancy. This may overshadow your feelings of excitement and anticipation. Your apprehension may inhibit bonding to the new baby during the pregnancy out of fear of another loss or disappointment. Usually once you are beyond the first trimester this anxiety decreases significantly. You will probably find that talking about these feelings with your medical caregiver and others who have had similar experiences can help to lessen your fears. Studies have shown that frequent visits to your medical caregiver early in pregnancy can help reduce anxiety, as can self-help groups or counseling.

Whatever your reaction, it is important to be honest with and kind to yourself. Get the support you need so you can move through another pregnancy without uncontrolled fear and anxiety, but with hope and courage.

Adoption

Not flesh of my flesh,
Not bone of my bone,
But still miraculously
my own
Never forget for a
single minute.

You didn't grow
Under my heart—
but in it.

Fleur Conkling Heyliger

Once you have worked through your feelings of loss and sadness about your miscarriage and examined your feelings about possible future pregnancies, you might decide, as many couples do, to seek out adoption as an alternative way of building your family. Adoption can be a welcome option, but there are a number of things to consider about it.

Adoption might be an acceptable way of becoming a parent for one of you but not the other. It is good to realize and accept this before beginning the adoption process. Your age or family circumstances might be factors in your decision to adopt. Sometimes adoption can be expensive, which might be another consideration. Be aware, too, that the process can be long, depending on the child you choose to adopt.

When considering adoption, it is important to investigate the agencies in your area to determine the availability of children, the costs, and other information. Contact several agencies to learn about their procedures, availability of children, and fees. Usually agencies have informational meetings at which you can have most of your questions answered. Other adoptive parents can be a valuable source of information and support. If you choose to adopt, it is important to recognize that it is a unique and

41

different way of becoming a parent. It is obviously not the same as giving birth, but it can be a welcome and desireable way of expanding or building your family.

Childlessness

Whether they [the childless couple] choose[s] to adopt or to channel their creativity and nurturing gifts elsewhere, they can find some measure of fulfillment, even though they may be unable to ever entirely cease mourning for their baby...

Mary Burgwyn

When another pregnancy is not possible, or if you choose not to try again, you might find it difficult to accept the reality of not having the children you had hoped for.

When parenthood by birth is not a choice it is common to feel not only the loss of the miscarried baby, but also the loss of your fertility, future, sexuality, "womanhood," or "manhood." As you face these realities you might experience feelings of sorrow, depression, anger, and despair. Coming to terms with these feelings can sometimes be a long and difficult process.

If you or your partner have children from a previous marriage, you might be very disappointed that you are not able to expand your new family as you had hoped and planned. You might find that others minimize this miscarriage because "after all, you already have children." The desire to have a child is a natural consequence of your loving relationship and the feelings you have for your partner. You might have dreams of having a specific number of children and the inability to have another child can be devastating. Although difficult, you will probably need to accept the reality that your family will have one child less than you desire.

If you have no children now, you might be forced to consider remaining childless. Although we live in a society that is very pro-child, many couples today are childless, whether by choice or chance. You, like others, can find life satisfying without children, especially if you are able to become involved in "giving" activities. These could be through your profession, religious work, volunteer work, or interactions with children. You might worry that you will be lonely, especially in your later years. Close relationships with other family members, such as nieces and nephews, can fill this void. In fact, studies have shown that childless couples, when compared with couples who have children, are as satisfied or more satisfied with their lives.

Childlessness may not be your first choice. However, it need not be chosen with resignation or discouragement. It can be a creative and positive decision.

Reproductive Technology

Questions now exist that would have seemed like flights of fancy a decade ago...We are constantly amazed at what [technology] produces, and in our slack-jawed wonder, we sometimes forget to look CRITICALLY at what we are marveling at, and we forget to ask how it will affect the quality of our lives.

Margot Fromer

Today there are new and revolutionary ways of giving birth to babies. Forms of reproductive technology such as in vitro fertilization (test tube babies), embryo transfer, artificial insemination, donor uterus, and surrogate motherhood have brought the possibility of "birth" children to couples who previously would not have been able to bear children. Such alternatives can be exciting and promising options that reflect modern technological advances. Or these options can seem strange, invasive, and unnatural.

Many of the alternatives currently available are experimental and sometimes expensive. The decision to use these methods is not an easy one. Therefore, explore your feelings and values carefully and educate yourself about the legal and ethical dimensions of each procedure before making a decision.

Unfortunately, the legal and religious communities have not kept pace with technology, and there are few laws that govern and protect those involved in birth through reproductive technology. You may find few religious guidelines to help you in your decision-making, except for a rejection of "unnatural" means of creating babies.

Try to think about future implications and the child's right to know the circumstances of his or her conception and birth. These issues are complex and there are no easy answers. Reproductive technology can be an alternative to childlessness if you and your partner consider it carefully and come to an agreement with which you are comfortable. It is a choice that you have, to choose or to reject.

****

Looking into the future and making decisions after a loss can feel overwhelming. Be careful about making major decisions too soon or before you are ready. It is wise to take your time and think things through.

It might be helpful to try to imagine what you would like your life to be like in five or ten years. Ask yourself what things would help or hinder you in reaching those dreams. Usually it is fairly easy to determine what might get in the way of achieving your future plans. It may be more helpful, although more difficult, to think about what resources you have or need for creating the future of your dreams. You may find that by imagining yourself in your future you are better able to see what goals are most important to you, what you value most in your life, and what you are willing and able to do to achieve your goals.

The challenge you face as you consider your future may be recognizing your alternatives. Whether you have alot of choices or only a few, realizing that you do have choices can be an important way to maintain or regain control of your own situation. It is also important to recognize your resources. Don't forget to take stock of what you have, whatever it is: satisfying relationships, spirituality, economic security, talents, or skills to suggest only a few. Even though you have experienced a loss, try to remember what you have and where you are going when making decisions that will be right for you.

6

Putting It In Perspective

We must always have old memories, and young hopes.
Arsene Houssaye

You have experienced a miscarriage and now must try to put it in perspective in your life. There are no "right" answers, no easy solutions, no best way to get through it. It is an experience uniquely yours. You can share it, but only you can move through it. It sometimes can feel like a very lonely experience, whether you accept your miscarriage easily or have a hard time accepting it.

There will be times when the memory of your baby is more painful than others—the anniversary of the miscarriage or the due date, during another pregnancy, or as you watch your children or other children grow older. Sometimes the trigger for your sadness may be something you can identify with like a TV commercial, a picture, or something you purchased in preparation for the baby. Other times the trigger may be more elusive and you find your tears there, unannounced and unpredicted. Don't be frightened or alarmed, for this is very normal. Memories can be a comfort but they can also, sometimes be painful. Subsequent bouts of sadness do not stay as long as when the sadness was new, but it visits every now and then, like an old acquaintance.

Perhaps you did not feel any great sadness at the time of your miscarriage but discover feelings of disapointment in the future. This is not as strange as it may seem. As your life changes and you move on, your remembrances and feelings about the miscarriage might also change.

As you put this experience in perspective in your life, you may find you have changed and grown in positive ways. The miscarriage can easily be bittersweet. Perhaps communication with your partner has become more open, maybe you have become more compassionate for others who experience pain, or you may have gained a greater appreciation for birth, life, or your other children.

This loss has now become a part of your life. It is something you will live with. Whether it is a significant or minor experience to you, in time it will become an old memory. Remember, life goes on—always moving, ever changing— presenting new opportunities, new joy and new hope. You need not dwell on your memories but you might find they will help you deal with your future and what lies ahead.

Have faith in yourself and your feelings. Be gentle with yourself. And most of all, have hope for tomorrow.

Index

Support and Resources

A Place to Remember 1885 Univ. Ave., #110 St. Paul, MN 55104 (800) 631-0973. Sells birth/death announcement cards, comfort/sympathy cards, anniversary cards, baby mementos and literature on perinatal loss. www.aplacetoremember.com

Babies Remembered 801 Twelve Oaks Center Drive Suite 803, Wayzata, MN 55391 (952) 476-1303. Sells books, booklets, audio-visuals, and ha,s consultant-trainer on infant loss and general bereavement. Offers poetry, sharing corner, updates, studies, support, and a newsletter. www.babiesremembered.org

Center for Loss in Multiple Birth, Inc.(CLIMB) PO Box 91377 Anchorage, AK 99509 (907) 222-5321. Support network by and for parents who have experienced the death of one or more babies from a twin or higher multiple pregnancy, during pregnancy, at or after birth or in childhood. c1imb@pobox.alaska.net www.climb-support.org

Centering Corporation 7230 Maple Street, Omaha, NE 68134 (866) 218-0101. Sells literature on death, dying and coping with bereavement issues, including divorce, illness, disability, death of children, adults and pets. www.centering.org

Compassion Books 7036 State Hwy 80 S., Burnsville, NC 28714 (828) 675-5909. A resource organization providing networking, training and resources related to loss and grief, death and dying, comfort and hope. www.compassionbooks.com

Compassionate Friends, Inc. (National Office) PO Box 3696, Oak Brook, IL 60522 (630) 990-0010 or (877) 969-0010. A self-help organization for families that experience a death of a child. Newsletter and many local support groups. www.compassionatefriends.org.

Compassionate Friends of Canada 685 Williams Ave., Winnipeg, Manitoba, Canada R3E OZ2. Mutual assistance groups for bereaved parents and siblings for the loss of a child at any age.

Group B Strep Association Offers support and information to create awareness, promote testing and treatment of GBS and to generate vaccine research. http://www.groupbstrep.org www.groupbstrepinternational.org

Pen-Parents of Australia PO 574, Belconnen, ACT 2626, Australia
Pen-Parents of Canada, RPO Box 52548, Coquitlam, BC V3B 7J4 Canada
Correspondence network for parents who have had a baby or child die.

First Candle/SIDS Alliance 1314 Bedford Ave. Suite 210, Baltimore, MD 21208 (800) 221-7437. Responds to parents, families, professionals and the general public seeking information and support on stillbirth and SIDS. Publications and newsletter. www.firstcandle.org

Hygeia Provides programs to educate, counsel, and support families who grieve the loss of a pregnancy or newborn child, advocate for healthcare of women and children worldwide www.hygeiafoundation.org

MISS (Mothers in Sympathy and Support) PO Box 5333 Peoria, AZ 85385-5333 (623) 979-1000. Helps families who have had a stillbirth or early infant death through local support groups, camps for grieving kids, resources, newsletters, and web site. www.missfoundation.org

SANDS, Promotes awareness and understanding following the death of a baby from conception through infancy. Newsletters, provides links to regional support groups, offers support, training, and resources. Australia: www.sands.org.au
New Zealand: www.sands.org.nz   UK: www.uk-sands.org

INFERTILITY

Hannah's Prayer PO Box 5016, Auburn, CA 95604. An organization with Christian emphasis, concentrating on infertility or the loss of a child any time from conception through infancy. Local support chapters, newsletter and penpals. www.hannah.org

RESOLVE, Inc. 7910 Woodmount Ave., Suite 1350, Bethesda, MD 20014 (888) 623-0744. Support, resources, education and information concerning infertility. Publishes newsletter and has many local chapters. www.resolve.org

ADOPTION

National Adoption Center 1500 Walnut St., #701, Philadelphia, PA 19102 (800) 862-3678. Information and referral service for special needs adoption. Offers state resource lists of adoption agencies, parent and advocacy groups. The Adoption Exchange matches families looking to adopt children with special needs. www.adopt.org

National Adoption Information Clearinghouse 1250 Maryland Ave. SW, 8th Floor, Washington DC 20024 (888) 251-0075. Distributes info. on all areas of adoption. email: naicinfo@erols.com Web Page http://www.niac.acf.hhs.gov

Websites for families

www.aplacetoremember.com
www.babiesremembered.org
http://sids-network.org
www.storknet.comlcubbies/pil/losspanel.htm
http://angels4ever.comlMultiples
http://pages.i village.com/pp/klaasje
http://members.tripod.com/-Neofight
www.climb-support.org
www.babyloss.com
www.pregnancy and infantloss.org
www.bonniebabes.org.au
www.stillbirthalliance.org

www.wintergreenpress.com
www.babyloss.com
www.hannah.org
http://griefnet.org
www.misschildren.org
www.angels4ever.com
www.angelnames.org
www.spals.com
www.sands.org.nz
www.sands.org.au
www.u.k.-sands.org

Bibliography

Bereaved Parent Support

After a Loss in Pregnancy, *Help for Families Affected by a Miscarriage, a Stillbirth or the Loss of a Newborn*, Nancy Berezin, Simon and Schuster, 1982/1990. Based on hundreds of interviews with women who have experienced losses, the book takes an honest look at a woman's grief and at the various social forces and institutions that work for or against recovery.

After the Loss of your Baby: For Teen Mothers, Connie Nykiel, For Teen Moms Only, PO Box 962, Frankfort, IL 60423, (815) 464-5465, 1996. A non-judgmental booklet filled with wisdom and good solid advice, as well as explanations of medical terms that may be new to a teen.

The Anguish of Loss, Julie Fritsch with Sherokee Ilse, Wintergreen Press, 1988/1997. The ultimate resource to sensitize all those who want to understand the turbulence of loss and grief. This journey, through a mother's sculptures and prose after her son's death, transcends cultures, language, history and time itself.

Another Baby? Maybe. Thirty Most Frequently Asked Subsequent Pregnancy Questions, Sherokee Ilse and Maribeth W. Doerr, Wintergreen Press. The authors, who have lived through a number of pregnancies after their own losses, share the most common concerns, issues and questions parents face when considering another pregnancy and living through it.

Comfort Us Lord—Our Baby Died, Rev. Norman Hagley, Centering Corp. A tender book of prayers for families whose baby has died, including miscarriage.

Comforting Those Who Grieve, Doug Manning, In-Sight Books. This practical book offers caring ways to help those in mourning. Common sense and a deep faith are blended in this insightful guide.

Coping with Infant or Fetal Loss: The couple's healing process, Kathleen Gilbert, Ph.D. and Laura Smart, Ph.D., Brunner/Mazel Publishers, 1992. Offers specific and useful suggestions for helping couples resolve their grief and reduce stress on their relationship, along with other valuable advice.

Coping with Holidays and Celebrations, Sherokee Ilse, Wintergreen Press. This booklet examines the difficulty one faces on holidays or at family gatherings after the loss of a child and offers suggestions to turn those days of difficulty toward inner reflection and even celebration of the child.

Don't Take My Grief Away From Me, Doug Manning, In-Sight Books Inc., PO Box 2058, Hereford, TX 79045. An excellent practical, supportive and informative book for grieving family members.

Empty Arms: *Coping with Miscarriage, Stillbirth and Infant Death*, Sherokee Ilse, Wintergreen Press, 1982/2002/2013. A unique and encouraging book reaching out to all who have been touched by infant death. Shared with families in hospitals and clinics across the nation, this compassionate guide invites bereaved parents to make their own choices and decisions. Available in **SPANISH.**

A Guide For Fathers, Tim Nelson, A Place to Remember, 2004/2007. The author shares his experience after his daughter's stillbirth, then adds his 10 year perspective on what went well, how he grieved and healed. One of the very few resources that deals openly and honestly with grief from a dad's view.

For Better or Worse, For Couples Whose Child Has Died, Maribeth Wilder Doerr, Centering Corp, 1992. A short, but helpful guide to better understand common reactions by men and women, offering encouragement to communicate and understanding.

From Sorrow to Serenity, Susan Fletcher, Hunter House Publications, 1998. Biblical daily affirmations to support families whose baby has died.

Healing Together: *For Couples Grieving the Death of Their Baby,* Marcia Tister and Sandia Torrell, Centering Corp., 1991. For couples whose baby dies, a book that covers memorial services to communication. Ends with "Letting Grief Strengthen Your Relationship."

Help, Comfort & Hope after Losing Your Baby in Pregnancy or the First Year, Hannah Lothrop, Fisher Books, 1997. Speaks to bereaved parents in the first section offering practical coping support and and the second section provides information for caregivers in the hospital and those professionals providing care for the family.

Infertility: *The Emotional Journey*, Michelle Fryer Hanson, Fairview Publishing, 1994. Stories of individuals' struggles with infertility, exploring different treatment options, family dynamics, and other emotional components.

Making it Through the Night, Pat Quidley and Marilyn Shroyer, Ph.D. For couples who are going through a tragic time. Gentle and affirming. This book guides you through the painful progression of feelings a crisis generates.

Men and Grief: *A Guide for Men Surviving the Death of a Loved One,* Carol Staudacher, New Harbinger Publications, 1991. Explores and identifies the major characteristics of men's grief, how they cope and facilitate their grief as well as presents examples or how to take care of themselves in grief.

Mending the Torn Fabric: *For Those Who Grieve and Those Who Want to Help them,* Sarah Brabant, Baywood Publishing Company, 1996. Professionally competent in its theoretical framework yet simple enough for the lay person, this is a compassionate accounting of the one of the most basic issues in life, the grieving process.

Miscarriage: *A Shattered Dream,* Sherokee Ilse and Linda Hammer Burns, Wintergreen Press, 1985/2002/2014. A comprehensive, sensitive guide on miscarriage—the medical and emotional aspects. Short, comprehensive, with a personal touch to a sensitive subject, given out in hospitals and clinics.

Miscarriage, Joy and Marv Johnson, Centering Corporation, 1988. This booklet deals with the validity of feelings, the value of the loss, family relationships and marital issues. (also available in Spanish)

Miscarriage: *A Man's Book,* Rick Wheat, Centering Corporation, 1995. Written by a marriage and family therapist who has experienced the difficulties of miscarriage first hand, it begins with an emergency page (items a man should know right away when his wife has a miscarriage).

Miscarriage—*Women Sharing from the Heart,* Marie Alen and Shelly Marks, Wiley Press, 1993. Available from ICEA. Comprehensive and human, with personal stories, suggestions and research on feelings.

Mother Care: *Physical Care and Beyond After a Baby Dies,* Sherokee Ilse, Inez Anderson and Mary Funk, Wintergreen Press. A 20 page guide for new mothers on how to care for themselves after their baby dies. Focuses on the physical area of healing, but emotional and spiritual aspects are also discussed. Important to be given to newly bereaved mothers immediately.

Oscaso Sin Aurora, Marta Steifel Ayala and Marie Ford, Centering Corp. A Spanish short guide after miscarriage & infant death.

Planning A Precious Goodbye, Sherokee Ilse and Susan Erling Martinez, Wintergreen Press. Short, comprehensive guide for writing an obituary, sending birth/death announcements, planning a funeral for babies, including miscarriage. Songs, poems, prose, readings and scripture.

Premature Babies: *A Handbook for Parents*, Sherry Nance, Arbor House, 1982. This comprehensive guide provides personal stories, practical advice and the latest medical findings, written by parents.

Preventing Miscarriage—The Good News, Jonathon Scher, MD and Carol Dix, Harper & Row, 1990. Information on why some pregnancies fail, new medical tests to pinpoint potential causes, and latest treatments available to prevent some losses in pregnancies. Not a cure all, but good information.

Remembering with Love: *Messages of Hope for the First Year of Grieving and Beyond*, Elizabeth Levang, Ph.D. and Sherokee Ilse, Fairview Press, 1992. An uplifting, daily affirmation book based on real scenarios of people who have had a loved one die. A readers guide at the beginning offers assistance in locating the topic or issue being faced at the moment.

A Silent Sorrow: Pregnancy Loss, Guidance and Support for You and Your Family, Ingrid Kohn, MSW and Perry-Lynn Moffitt, Dell, 1993. Covers most aspects of pregnancy loss in a compassionate manner (over 400 pages). Excellent for families and care providers.

Single Parent Grief, Sherokee Ilse, A Place to Remember. For teens or a more mature parent, this resource explores the special grief of single parents who have no steady partner. Suggestions and information offer hope, a good resource section included.

Surviving Pregnancy Loss, Rochelle Friedman, MD, Bonnie Gradstein, MD, Little Brown & Co., 1982. The book provides a comprehensive discussion of the physical and emotional consequences of pregnancy loss.

Tender Miscarriage: An Epiphany, Paula Saffire, Harbinger House, 1989. A gentle story of love and loss written to the little baby who died and the millions who share such a tragic journey.

Transcending Loss: *Understanding the Lifelong Impact of Grief and How to Make it Meaningful*, Ashley Davis Prend, Berkely Books, 1997. One of the few books that gives support for the importance of grief's ongoing impact and how it changes through the years.

Unsupported Losses: *Blighted Ovum, Ectopic and Molar Pregnancies*, Sherokee Ilse, A Place to Remember. These losses are often misunderstood and there is little written on them. This booklet addresses the complicating factors surrounding these losses, offering emotional support and an understanding of medical implications.

When Hello Means Goodbye, Pat Schwiebert and Paul Kirk, Perinatal Loss, 1977. One of the first booklets written for bereaved families, practical and full of advice from people who have been there.

A Woman Doctor's Guide to Miscarriage: *Essential facts and Up-to-the Minute Information on Coping with Pregnancy Loss and Trying Again,* Irene Daria, Laurie Abkemeier, Lynn Friedman, vol. 1, 1996, available from amazon.com on the internet.

Helping Children Cope

Answers to a Child's Questions about Death, Peter Stellman, Guideline Publishers, Stamford, NY 12167, available from ICEA (612) 854-8660, 1990. Contains sketches, questions and answers designed to be read with children.

Helping Children Cope with the Loss of a Loved One, Dr. William Koren, Free Spirit Press, 1996. In concise language, the author offers comfort, compassion and sound advice. He explains how children from infancy - 18 perceive and react to death with suggestions to help children live through loss.

How Do We Tell the Children: *A Parent's Guide to Helping Children Understand and Cope When Someone Dies,* Don Schaefer and Christine Lyons, New Market Press, NY, 1994. Provides straight forward, uncomplicated language that will help parents explain death to children from two years to the teenage years.

Keys to Helping Children Deal with Death and Grief, Joy Johnson, Barron's Educational Services, NY, 1999. Well written, sensitive and full of advice for parents and others who lovingly interact with children.

Lifetimes: *A Beautiful Way to Explain Death to Children,* Bryan Mellonie and Robert Ingpen, Bantam Books, 1983. Explains how all living things have beginnings and endings.

Molly's Rosebush, Janice Cohn, Albert Whitman & Co., 1995. One of the nicest children's books available on miscarriage. Fully illustrated in pastels, this real life story openly confronts the fears that might affect siblings after a miscarriage.

No New Baby, Marilyn Bryte, Centering Corp., 1988. For siblings when a baby brother or sister dies through miscarriage.

Our Baby Died. Why? Susan Erling Martinez and Jake Erling, A Place to Remember, 1984/1996. Jake, the surviving older brother shares his thoughts, fears, feelings and questions after the stillbirth of his baby brother.

Sibling Grief, Sherokee Ilse, Linda H. Burns, Wintergreen Press. A practical guide to help parents understand their surviving children's needs, assisting them in grieving and coping with their brother or sister's death.

Thumpy's Story: *A Story of Love and Grief Shared*, Nancy Dodge, SHARE, 1985. A story book, workbook, and video that tells a story of a sibling bunny's death in a very gentle and understanding way.

Where's Jess? Centering Corp. An excellent book for siblings after their neonatal baby brother or sister dies.

Pregnancy Complications

Every Pregnant Woman's Guide to Preventing Preterm Birth, Barbara Like, Times Books, 1995. Practical, scientifically sound information on risk factors identified with prematurity and how to reduce them.

How to Prevent Miscarriages and Other Crises of Pregnancy, Stefan Semchyshyn, MD and Carol Colman, Collier, 1990. Addresses some causes of miscarriage and premature labor, then offers sound, state of the art advice on potential treatment options.

Precious Lives, Painful Choices: *A Prenatal Decision-Making Guide*, Sherokee Ilse, Wintergreen Press, 1993/2005. Comprehensive, balanced guide to assist families in their struggle with abnormal prenatal results. To be given immediately upon diagnosis to aid in decision-making.

When Pregnancy Isn't Perfect, Laurie Rich, Dutton Books, 1991. A layperson's guide to complications in pregnancy, written by a mother who went through a high-risk pregnancy. Deals with medical and emotional.

For an even more comprehensive and up-to-date bibliography, contact *A Place to Remember* and ask to buy their Resource List and Bibliography. (800) 631-0973 1885 University Ave. Suite 110, St. Paul, MN 55104. www.aplacetoremember.com

A Note From The Authors

We would very much like to hear your comments about this book. Also, feel free to share your suggestions for improvement and any personal stories. Thank you for your interest in *Miscarriage: A Shattered Dream.* Please write to:

Miscarriage
801 Twelve Oaks Center Drive Suite 803
Wayzata, MN 55391
952-476-1303

Visit www.wintergreenpress.com to see dozens of resources to help you at this time and over time.

Other Resources By Wintergreen Press

EMPTY ARMS: Coping with Miscarriage, Stillbirth and Infant Loss, Sherokee Ilse $12.95

Newly revised! 2013. This sensitive, classic guide is given to thousands of families by hosiptals, clinics, funeral directors, clergy, family and friends throughout the country. Sherokee is like a friend, reaching out to offer guidance in the hours, days, weeks, and months that follow the loss of a baby.
Bulk rate available.

THE ANGUISH OF LOSS, Julie Fritsch with Sherokee Ilse $14.95

A powerful, emotional journey through loss and grief, this most unique book teaches people like nothing else. Minimal use of prose and clay sculptures tell the story of a mother's loss. All who have experienced loss will find help and be able to relate–whether miscarriage, infant death, other deaths, divorce, or job loss.